LOVE YOUR RABBIT

YOUR RABBIT

Judith Heneghan

WAYLAND

First published in 2012 by Wayland

Copyright © Wayland 2012

Wayland
338 Euston Road
London NW1 3BH

Wayland Australia
Level 17/207 Kent Street
Sydney, NSW 2000

Editor: Nicola Edwards
Designer: Rocket Design (East Anglia) Ltd
Picture researcher: Nicola Edwards

The consultant, Anna Claxton, has worked
for some of the UK's largest animal welfare
charities since 2003, and as a lecturer in animal
welfare and animal care. She has an MSc in
Applied Animal Behaviour and Animal Welfare.

British Library Cataloguing in Publication Data

Heneghan, Judith.
 Love your rabbit. -- (Your perfect pet)
 1. Rabbits--Juvenile literature.
 I. Title II. Series
 636.8-dc23

ISBN: 978 0 7502 6893 6

Printed in China

Wayland is a division of Hachette Children's
Books, an Hachette UK company

www.hachette.co.uk

Picture Acknowledgements: The author and publisher
would like to thank the following for allowing their
pictures to be reproduced in this publication:
Cover (main) Shutterstock © fivespots, (inset) iStock ©
Pamela Moore; title page iStock © Pamela Moore; p4
(tl) Shutterstock © muzsy, (tr) Shutterstock © fivespots,
(b) Shutterstock © Iakov Filimonov; p5 Shutterstock ©
Eric Esselée; p6 RSPCA Philip Toscano; p7 (t) Becky
Murray/RSPCA, (b) Shutterstock © Eric Esselée; p8
Shutterstock © cameilia; p9 (t) RSPCA Andrew Forsyth,
(b) Shutterstock © Kapu; p10 RSPCA Angela Hampton;
p11 (t) Shutterstock © xjrshimada, (b) Shutterstock
© Nick Biemans; p12 © Cultura Creative/Alamy; p13
(t) iStock © Carl Domke, (b) Shutterstock © misha
shiyanov; p14 (t) Shutterstock ©AnetaPics, (b) RSPCA
Joe Murphy/RSPCA; p15 RSPCA Philip Toscano/
RSPCA; p16 RSPCA David Chapman; p17 (t) RSPCA
Philip Toscano/RSPCA, (b) Shutterstock ©WimL; p18
Shutterstock © foto ARts; p19 (t) iStock © Isabelle
Mory, (b) RSPCA Chris Brignell; p20 (t) RSPCA
1093398 Andrew Forsyth/RSPCA, (b) Shutterstock
©Dmitry Kalinovsky; p21 Shutterstock © foto Arts;
p22 RSPCA Damion Diplock/RSPCA; p23 (t) Alamy
© Tierfotoagentur/Alamy, (b) Shutterstock © Alan
Scheer; p24 Alamy ©Warwick Sloss/Alamy; p25 (t)
Shutterstock © Eric Esselée, (b) Shutterstock © M
Choco; p26 Shutterstock © Wallenrock; p27 (t) RSPCA
Joe Murphy/RSPCA, (b) Shutterstock © Eric Esselée;
p28) iStock © Pamela Moore ; p29 (t) Shutterstock
©Francesco83, (b) Shutterstock © fivespots

Contents

My pet rabbits 4

A safe home 6

A healthy diet 8

Warm and clean 10

Holding your rabbit 12

Running and hiding 14

Keeping active 16

Fur, teeth and nails 18

Visit the vet 20

All year round 22

Safety alert! 24

Getting older 26

Best friends 28

Quiz 30

Glossary 31

Index 32

3

My Pet Rabbits

I have two pet rabbits called Bubble and Squeak. Squeak is a bit bigger than Bubble. They are brother and sister, so they get on well. As they are boy and girl they have been neutered (see page 20). I love watching them hop around together.

Pet rabbits need the company of other rabbits as well as their human carers.

The big question...

Can I keep just one rabbit?

Rabbits need to be with their own kind. A rabbit on its own may feel bored or stressed. If you have one, and want to introduce a friend, ask your vet for advice to make sure they don't fight. Two rabbits will need plenty of space to get away from each other if they want to.

Rabbits are very cute and playful, but each year thousands end up at rescue centres because their owners didn't realise how much care and attention they needed. Make sure you think carefully before choosing a rabbit for a pet. This book will help you to find out if a rabbit is the right pet for you.

Pet power

There are many types, or breeds, of pet rabbit. Different breeds very a lot in appearance, but all pet rabbits are related to wild rabbits and show very similar behaviour.

Female rabbits are called does, the males are called bucks and their babies are called kits.

A Safe Home

Bubble and Squeak live outside in a special enclosure. It is big enough for them to run around and it has separate areas for sleeping, eating and going to the toilet. It takes up quite a lot of space!

An enclosure needs to be tall enough for your rabbits to stand up on their hind legs without touching the roof.

The big question...

Can rabbits live indoors?
Some people prefer to keep their rabbits indoors. Indoor rabbits still need a shelter and plenty of room for exercise, with no access to dangers such as electric cables, poisonous plants or other pets such as cats and dogs. They will also need somewhere to go to the toilet, such as a tray filled with hay or newspaper.

Your rabbits need a safe and secure shelter inside their enclosure. The shelter has to be warm, dry and big enough for your pets to lie down fully stretched out. It should also be raised off the ground to stop it getting damp. The rabbits should to be able to move in and out of it whenever they want.

An outdoor shelter or hutch needs to be attached to the run and be off the ground. It should protect your rabbits from the sun, wind and rain.

Furry facts

Young rabbits reach their adult size at about five months. The rabbit shown here is five weeks old. If you buy baby rabbits, find out how big they are likely to grow and make sure your run and shelter are big enough. Two rabbits will need more space than one rabbit.

A Healthy Diet

Bubble and Squeak's favourite food is hay and they munch loads of it every day. They like green vegetables too, especially broccoli and celery. Carrots are only for treats as they are more fattening. I wash the vegetables first and feed them every morning and evening.

Green vegetables form part of a healthy diet for a rabbit.

The big question...

Should I give my rabbits muesli?

Rabbits are fussy eaters, so muesli isn't good for them as they waste the bits they don't like. To make sure your rabbits get everything they need, give them plenty of hay and a handful of raw green vegetables every day. You can also add some good quality rabbit pellets.

Rabbits need plenty of fresh water, and like to drink from a bowl. It should be heavy enough so that your rabbits won't tip it over. You could also try a water bottle with a metal spout attached to the side of the enclosure. Remember to change the water every day.

Rabbits need access to fresh water at all times.

Rabbits should have a constant supply of hay.

Pet power

Wild rabbits spend most of their time eating grass. Pet rabbits eat hay, which is dried grass. Hay needs a lot of chewing, which stops the rabbits getting bored. It also keeps their insides and teeth healthy.

Warm and Clean

Rabbits need a warm, clean shelter for sleeping and hiding. Bubble and Squeak like snuggling up in a bed of fresh dry straw. Underneath the straw there's a layer of newspaper. This makes their shelter really cosy. I change the straw and the newspaper each week.

The big question...

Why does my rabbit eat its droppings?

Grass and hay are natural foods for rabbits, but they are hard to digest. Sometimes rabbits eat their own droppings so that they pass through their bodies a second time. This is to make sure they get all the goodness they can from their food. It is quite normal and nothing to worry about.

Rabbits are very clean animals and wash their fur carefully with their tongue. They don't need a bath unless they are ill and can't clean themselves. If your rabbit looks dirty, particularly around its bottom, it may be a sign that it is unwell and you should speak to your vet.

Rabbits lick their paws and rub them over their ears to keep them clean.

Pet power

Rabbits in the wild live in underground tunnels called burrows. A burrow provides shelter from the cold, and protection from larger animals such as foxes and eagles. Rabbits make sleeping nests inside the burrows, lining them with dried grass and even some of their own fur.

Wild rabbits come out of their burrow to look for food.

Holding your Rabbit

When Bubble and Squeak first came to live with us, they were still young. They seemed nervous when I tried to hold them. I had to be patient until they'd learned to trust me. Now when I call their names they hop over to say hello. They don't mind being picked up, and they love it when I tickle them behind their ears!

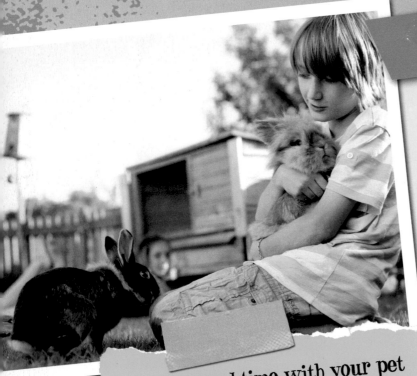

If you spend time with your pet rabbits, they will learn to enjoy your company.

The big question...

Why does my rabbit scratch me?

If your rabbits don't like to be held, be patient. Talk quietly and try putting treats on your hand. When they trust you, they will be calmer. If you handle them, make sure their bottom is supported as they have fragile spines. All four paws should be against your body.

In the wild, rabbits are hunted by animals that are larger than them. So rabbits often feel nervous near bigger animals, like us! They won't want you holding them at first, so try sitting down next to them until they are used to your smell and your voice.

If your rabbit is nervous, use both hands to hold it in your lap while sitting on the ground. Then, if it wriggles free, it won't hurt itself.

Pet power

Rabbits have large, sensitive ears and excellent hearing. They warn other rabbits of approaching danger by thumping the ground with their back legs.

Running and Hiding

Bubble and Squeak are fast movers! They love hopping around their grassy run but if they are frightened by a sudden noise or a stranger, they dash for their shelter. I've put a hollow plastic tube and an old box in the enclosure so they now have extra places to hide.

Help your rabbits feel safe by giving them lots of places to hide.

The big question...

Why does my friend's rabbit 'freeze' when I go near it?

In the wild, rabbits are prey for bigger animals. Predators such as buzzards hunt them by looking for movement. So when a rabbit thinks danger is near it either runs and hides or stands completely still. If your friend's rabbit 'freezes', try backing away and talk gently to it so that it learns you're not a threat.

Have you ever seen a rabbit in the wild running in zig zags? If a rabbit is being chased it will try to avoid capture by quickly changing direction. Rabbits are fast and agile. Their back legs are very powerful and if danger comes too close they may use them to kick in self defence. If your pet rabbit kicks, it may be feeling frightened.

Rabbits have strong back legs for running, leaping and kicking.

Furry facts

Rabbits in the wild can run at speeds of up to 45 miles per hour over short distances. Pet rabbits tend to be a bit slower, but they can still sprint when they want to!

Keeping Active

Bubble and Squeak need to dig and explore. I give them something new to investigate every week. They like logs to hop on, cardboard boxes to hide in and balls to nudge with their noses. Bubble's favourite is a hollow cardboard tube stuffed with hay. She loves to tug out the hay and eat it.

Rabbits are excellent diggers. In the wild, they live with other rabbits in a series of connected tunnels called a warren.

The big question...

Will my rabbits dig a tunnel and escape?

If your rabbits' run is outdoors, sink the frame into the ground so that they can't dig underneath the sides. However, do remember that digging is part of their natural behaviour. You can help them by providing a deep tray filled with soil inside their run. Then they can dig safely!

Rabbits are intelligent animals and get bored, just like we do. To stop your rabbits getting bored, change their toys regularly. Old toys can be put away and brought out again in a few weeks. Remember to give them a wash at the same time.

Whether your rabbits live outdoors or indoors, they need toys to play with and a tray for digging.

Furry facts

Rabbits see best in the dim half-light of dawn and dusk. This is when they are most active. However, it isn't always easy to tell if your rabbits are awake as they can sleep with their eyes open!

Fur, Teeth and Nails

Bubble and Squeak have amazing teeth; they never stop growing! Luckily they chew lots of rough hay, which helps grind their teeth down. I check their gums every week, just to make sure their teeth aren't causing problems. If a rabbit's teeth grow too long it will have a very sore mouth.

The big question...

What should I do if my rabbit's nails grow too long?

Rabbit nails should be checked regularly and may need clipping to keep them short. Get an experienced adult to do this for you.

Rabbits that live indoors on soft carpets and smooth flooring will need to have their nails clipped regularly.

Rabbits may spend several hours a day chewing hay. This is just what their teeth need.

Rabbits use their tongues to lick themselves clean. However, this can lead to a dangerous build-up of hair inside their stomachs. It is a good idea to groom short-haired rabbits with a soft brush once a week to remove old fur and keep their coats healthy. Long-haired rabbits will need brushing more often.

Furry facts

If a rabbit's teeth grow too long it can cause real suffering to the rabbit. It will probably stop eating. If you think there's a problem with your rabbit's teeth, take it to the vet for advice and treatment.

A rabbit's front teeth grow up to 3mm every week!

Visit the Vet

We take Bubble and Squeak to the vet for a check-up every six months. The vet nurse weighs them both and the vet gives them a vaccination. Vaccinations help protect pets from dangerous diseases. I give them a treat to nibble on afterwards!

A special travelling box is ideal for transporting your rabbit to the vet.

The big question...

What is neutering?

Neutering is when the vet performs an operation on your rabbit to stop it breeding and having babies. If you have a male and a female, make sure they are neutered before you put them together.

Sick rabbits will try to hide their illness for as long as they can because in the wild, a sick rabbit is easy prey for larger animals such as foxes. So it is important to check your rabbits regularly for any signs of illness. These might include being extra sleepy, eating less than usual, drinking more than usual, having dirty fur, sticky eyes or lumps under the skin.

A vet can give your rabbit regular check-ups and advise on the best time to have it neutered.

Furry facts

If male and female rabbits aren't neutered they will soon produce a litter of up to 15 babies or kits and you will have to find homes for them all! Females are also more likely to develop serious illness if they aren't neutered.

All Year Round

Never leave your rabbit in direct sunlight. A shady place is best.

Bubble and Squeak live outside in their enclosure for most of the year. In summer I make sure their shelter is in the shade to stop them getting hot. In the winter, when it gets very cold, my dad helps me move the shelter into our garden shed.

The big question...

What is fly strike?

Fly strike is a very serious condition caused by flies laying their eggs in a rabbit's dirty fur. The eggs hatch into maggots which feed on the rabbit's skin. Fly strike is more likely in warm weather, so during the summer you should check daily to make sure that the fur under your rabbit's tail is clean.

If your rabbits live outside and you are worried about the cold, provide them with extra bedding or place a rug or cover over the top of their shelter. Just make sure their drinking water doesn't freeze. Or you could move their shelter into an empty shed or garage. Don't keep your rabbits in the same place as a vehicle because exhaust fumes are highly poisonous.

Make sure your rabbits have extra bedding in cold weather.

Pet power
Rabbits do not hibernate during the cold winter months, but they may slow down a little as they try to save energy. You may also notice that their fur grows more thickly.

23

Safety Alert!

Bubble and Squeak love being outdoors, but they stay in their run. Our garden isn't a safe place for rabbits to explore freely. They might hop under the gate, or eat my mum's daffodils which would poison them. Instead we move their shelter and run around the garden so that they can experience it safely.

The big question...

My rabbits are safe from predators, aren't they?

Predators such as foxes and cats are clever creatures. They soon learn how to push through a narrow gap or lift a simple latch on a door. Make sure you lock the door of the shelter with a padlock or a metal bolt every time you close it.

If your garden is often visited by predators, bring your rabbits inside at night.

Indoor rabbits are safe from foxes, but they need to be protected from other hazards in your home. Electric cables are a real danger. Rabbits love to chew them, which may result in a severe electric shock. Keep house plants out of reach, too, as they could be poisonous for rabbits. Apple pips are also poisonous for them.

If you have other pets, such as cats and dogs, make sure they can't scare your rabbits.

Furry facts

Plants that are poisonous for rabbits include daffodils, tulips, lily-of-the-valley, amaryllis, oleander, bracken and most evergreen trees and shrubs. Never let your rabbit eat any unfamiliar plants.

Many common plants, such as tulips and daffodils, are poisonous for rabbits.

Getting Older

Bubble and Squeak are two years old now. They are healthy and active and I watch their diet to make sure they don't become overweight. Our vet says rabbits live longer if they stay fit and are well cared for. Older rabbits tend to slow down a bit but a balanced diet, good vet care and a safe, fun environment will help keep them active for longer.

The big question...

Why is my rabbit scratching its ears so much?

Rabbits can get ear mites, which cause itching and a build-up of sticky wax and dirt. If the insides of your rabbit's ears look dirty, don't try to clean it out yourself as you may damage the sensitive inner ear. Ask your vet's advice.

If you and your family go on holiday, ask a friend or neighbour to look after your rabbits until you get back. Aim to find someone who will come to your home and look after your rabbits just as you do. However, if you need to leave your pets in someone else's home, take their shelter, their toys and some of their old straw along as well. This will help your rabbits settle in.

If you go on holiday, leave instructions for the people who are taking care of your rabbits while you're away.

Furry facts

Pet rabbits that are well cared for can live for 8-12 years – some can live even longer.

This rabbit is five years old. Older rabbits may be more comfortable indoors in the warmth.

Best Friends

I love my rabbits Bubble and Squeak. Their noses always twitch when they see me, and they've learned to come when I call their names. They need lots of care and attention, but they're worth it - we have so much fun!

Pet power

Rabbits can be trained to do some things, such as to go to the toilet in a litter tray. Fill a plastic tray with torn up newspaper and place a few of your rabbit's droppings on top. Let your rabbit investigate, and reward it with a treat whenever it hops in and does its business.

My rabbits love being stroked. They are my best friends.

Rabbits communicate with each other mainly through smell. They have scent glands behind their tails and they mark their surroundings with scent as a way of leaving messages for each other. Your rabbit's nose twitches when it is trying to learn more about you.

A rabbit's whiskers are very sensitive; they help detect objects and obstacles.

Furry facts

Rabbits have an eye on each side of their head. This gives them good all-round vision for spotting bigger predator animals in the air above or behind them. It also means they have a blind spot directly in front of their noses!

Quiz

How well do you know rabbits?
Try this quick quiz to find out!

1. **Pet rabbits like to eat hay. How much should they munch each day?**

   a. A small handful
   b. As much as they like
   c. Five kilograms

2. **Rabbits have an eye on each side of the head. This means:**

   a. They can see predators behind and above them
   b. They can see two different things at once
   c. They don't have to look down their noses

3. **A rabbit's teeth never stop growing, but how quickly does this happen?**

   a. Three millimetres a day
   b. Three millimetres a week
   c. Three millimetres a year

4. **Some plants and foods are poisonous for rabbits. Which one is poisonous here?**

   a. Broccoli
   b. Celery
   c. Apple pips

5. **How do rabbits warn each other of approaching danger?**

   a. They thump the ground with their back legs
   b. They hop up and down
   c. They mark the ground with scent from their scent glands

6. **Why do rabbits twitch their noses?**

   a. To look cute
   b. To pick up scent from other animals
   c. To waggle their whiskers

Answers

1(b); 2(a); 3(b); 4(c); 5(a); 6(b)

Glossary

blind spot the area in front of a rabbit's nose which it can't see because of the position of its eyes

buck male rabbit

burrow a rabbit's underground home

digest the way food is broken down inside the gut

doe female rabbit

droppings rabbit poo

enclosure a secure area

environment surroundings

groom brush

hibernate sleep through the winter months

hind legs back legs

hutch a shelter for sleeping and keeping warm and dry

kits baby rabbits

litter tray a tray full of newspaper where rabbits can learn to go to the toilet

muesli a mix of oats and other grains

neutering an operation to stop a rabbit breeding and having kits

predator an animal that hunts other animals for food

prey an animal that is hunted for food

run a large enclosed area for outdoor exercise

vaccination an injection to prevent disease

warren an area of connecting underground burrows where lots of rabbits live

Index

appearance 5
attention 5, 28

bedding 10, 23, 27
behaviour 5
boredom 4, 9, 17
breeding 20
breeds 5
bucks 5
burrows 11

care 5, 28
communication 29

digging 16, 17
does 5
droppings 10, 28

ear mites 26
eating 6, 8, 10
enclosure 6, 7, 14, 22
energy 23
exercise 6
exploring 16

fly strike 22
freezing 14
fur 11, 19, 22, 23

going to the toilet 6, 28
grooming 19
gums 18

hay 6, 8, 9, 10, 16, 18, 19
healthy diet 8, 26
hearing 13
hiding 10, 14
holding, 12, 13
holidays 27

illness 11, 20, 21
indoor rabbits 6, 25
introducing another rabbit 4

kicking 15
kits 5, 21

litter tray 28

nails 18
neutering 4, 20, 21

older rabbits 26, 27

poisonous plants 24, 25
predators 13, 14, 24
prey 21

rabbit pellets 8
rescue centres 5
run 7, 14, 16, 24

safety 6, 23, 24, 25
scent glands 29
shelter 6, 7, 10, 11, 14, 22, 23, 27
signs of illness 21
sleeping 6, 10, 11
smell 29
space 4, 6, 7
speed 15
stress 4

tail 22, 29
teeth 18, 19
toys 16, 17, 27
training 28
treats 8, 12, 20, 28

vaccination 20
vegetables 8
vet 4, 11, 19, 20, 21, 26
vision 17, 29

warren 16
washing 11
water 9, 23
weather 7, 22, 23
whiskers 29
wild rabbits 5, 11, 13, 15, 16

The five welfare needs

In England and Wales it is the law that all pet owners must meet their pet's needs in the following way:

- a suitable place to live
- a proper diet with plenty of fresh water
- protection from and treatment of illness and injury
- allowed to behave normally
- housed with, or apart from, other animals according to their needs.

Owners who don't care for their pets in this way are breaking the law.
For more information, see http://www.rspca-eduction.org.uk/allaboutanimals/pets/rabbits

Contents of all the titles in the series:

YOUR PERFECT PET

Love Your Cat
978 0 7502 6892 9

A new kitten
Getting ready
Settling in
Food and water
Keeping clean
Good grooming
Playtime!
On the prowl
Safe at home
Vet check
Going away
Getting older
Best friends
Quiz
Glossary
Index

Love Your Hamster
978 0 7502 6894 3

My pet hamster
A place to live
Bedding and nesting
Night and day
Running and exploring
Food and water
Cheeky eaters
Holding your hamster
Keeping clean
Going away
Staying healthy
Getting older
Best friends
Quiz
Glossary
Index

Love Your Dog
978 0 7502 6891 2

A new puppy
Getting ready
Settling in
Food and water
Keeping clean
Vet check
Playtime!
Training fun
Off for a walk
Good grooming
Going away
Getting older
Best friends
Quiz
Glossary
Index

Love Your Rabbit
978 0 7502 6893 6

My pet rabbits
A safe home
A healthy diet
Warm and clean
Holding your rabbit
Running and hiding
Keeping active
Fur, teeth and nails
Visit the vet
All year round
Safety alert!
Getting older
Best friends
Quiz
Glossary
Index

WAYLAND